Isha on the Waves

Swapna Haddow

Illustrated by **Alessandra Santelli**

OXFORD
UNIVERSITY PRESS

I love proving people wrong, which made writing Ishi's story all the more important to me. I spent most of my childhood being told what I could and couldn't do, but it didn't stop me dreaming of a different life for myself. Eventually I learned that if I wanted to carve my own path, I would have to tell the world what I wanted. And you know what? Everyone who mattered supported me.

When someone underestimates you, I dare you to prove them wrong. Believing in myself is why I'm a writer today. Every day when I wake up, I can't quite believe I have the best job in the world.

Swapna Haddow

Chapter One

Ishi sat on the edge of her uncle's fishing boat, watching the waves roll in. She tucked her surfboard under her arm and swung her legs off the side of the boat. She was ready to jump off as soon as the boat came into the harbour.

'Bye, Amma,' Ishi yelled at her mother, who was untangling nets.

Ishi scrambled off the boat and raced towards the beach.

She spotted Adya's mum on the sand. Ishi's best friend, Adya, was already sitting out on the waves as Ishi paddled out.

'It's a bit gnarly today,' Adya said as Ishi joined her. The waves were choppy and powerful.

'It always is,' Ishi grinned back.

As a wave swept towards them, Ishi turned back towards the beach. She dipped the nose of her board down into the water. She paddled hard and then she lay still on her board. She shut her eyes and felt the water push her up.

Ishi remembered the years her aunty had spent teaching her to surf every morning before they went out on the fishing boats.

And then she heard her aunty's voice in her head.

Breathe.

Ishi took a breath and leaped to her feet. She balanced on the board as the water glided her back towards the shore.

She crouched low and let her hand carve up the wave as she surfed on to the sand.

'You were awesome out there!' Adya exclaimed.

'Excellent work, Ishi,' Adya's mum said.

Ishi beamed.

'Tell her, Mum,' Adya said, bouncing up and down. 'Tell her!'

Ishi raised her eyebrows as Adya's mum handed her a piece of paper.

'This would be perfect for you,' she said to Ishi.

Chapter Two

I shi unfolded the paper.
  'The National Junior Surfing
Competition is coming to Kerala?'

Adya exploded with excitement. 'And
look at the prize!'

A trip to Australia! That was Ishi's
dream. She'd spent years imagining
surfing around the world. Australia was
top of her list.

Ishi looked up at Adya's mum.

'You are good enough,' Adya's mum smiled. 'You could win this.'

Ishi stared down at the paper. The competition was at Lighthouse Beach. She'd surfed there before with her aunty, so it was special to Ishi. She knew the waves well.

'I'm going to enter,' she said.

Adya squealed and hugged her.

National Junior Surfing Competition

Lighthouse Beach

Chapter Three

Later that afternoon, Ishi headed home to talk to her mother. Ishi paced up and down, working out what to say. Her mother wasn't home yet so she had some time to think about it.

Her hand clenched around the flyer in her pocket. She knew she should have told her mother before she signed up to enter but she was afraid her mother would have said 'no'. She could imagine her mother saying, 'What about all your chores, Ishi? What about your schoolwork? You don't have time for competitions!'

At last, Ishi spotted her mother walking towards the house.

'Amma!' called Ishi. 'I need to ask you something!'

'It's too late to ask if you've already done it,' said Amma, brushing past Ishi.

Ishi's shoulders slumped as she followed after her mother. 'How did you find out?'

'The children from the surf club told me you'd entered your name for the competition tomorrow.'

Ishi swallowed hard. Her mother's voice was filled with hurt.

'I'm sorry,' Ishi whispered. 'I should've said something first.'

'We're supposed to make decisions like this together, Ishi,' said her mother sternly.

'I'm sorry,' Ishi insisted, but her apology was swallowed up by the slam of the bathroom door.

Ishi couldn't enter the competition now. She'd let her mother down so badly.

Chapter Four

Ishi felt like she'd barely slept when her alarm rang early the next morning. She dragged herself out of bed and got ready to head down to the beach to help her mother with her work.

'Amma?' she called out to her mother, as she approached their boat.

Ishi's mother was waxing a surfboard. As Ishi got closer, she recognized the hand-painted dolphins and yellow swirls on the surfboard. She used to sit on this board as a toddler – it was her aunty's competition surfboard.

'I hear you have a competition today,' Ishi's mother said. 'You'll need a board.'

'But yesterday – ' Ishi started.

Her mother patted the floor next to her, beckoning Ishi to sit.

'Yesterday, I was disappointed that you weren't honest with me.'

'I can't surf in this competition knowing you're disappointed in me,' Ishi said, sadly.

'And I can't let you pass up this opportunity,' her mother replied. 'Your aunty would be disappointed in *me*.'

Ishi brushed away a tear. 'I miss her so much.'

'I miss her too,' her mother said, hugging Ishi close. 'She would want you to surf today.'

'But what about my chores?' Ishi asked.

Her mother stood up and waved a hand. 'Don't worry about that.' She picked up the board. 'Adya's mum is waiting to take you to the competition.'

Chapter Five

'What happened to your foot?' Ishi exclaimed when she saw Adya's bandaged leg.

'I sprained my ankle,' Adya replied. 'You'll have to win this for the both of us,' she grinned at her friend.

Ishi loaded her surfboard into the back of the pickup truck and jumped in next to Adya.

'Ready to go?' Adya's mum asked the girls.

Ishi nodded. Her mouth felt dry and there was a fluttery feeling in the pit of her stomach, but she was ready to surf.

When they arrived at Lighthouse Beach, music was booming out. Lots of surfers were already out on the waves.

Ishi went up to the registration desk. The fluttery feeling got worse.

She was pointing out her name to the woman behind the desk when a judge approached the table.

'How old are you?' he asked.

'I'll be twelve soon,' she said.

'You're far too young for this competition,' he said, shaking his head.

'But there's no mention of an age limit on the sign-up form,' Adya's mum interrupted.

'The youngest competitor here is fourteen years old,' the judge argued. He glared at Ishi. 'You're simply too young.'

'I've been surfing these waves with my aunty since I was three years old,' Ishi exclaimed.

'And I'm sure you're quite good for your age,' he said, looking down his nose at Ishi. 'Perhaps think about entering again in a few years' time.'

He took Ishi's registration form and walked away, leaving Ishi at the table.

Chapter Six

'What is going on?' a voice called. 'Amma!' Ishi cried, running into her mother's arms. 'You're here.'

'They won't let Ishi compete,' Adya's mum sighed.

'But I came to watch Ishi surf,' Ishi's mother protested. 'And I brought some of her fans.'

Ishi saw a coach pull up and off stepped her friends, her teachers and her neighbours from the harbour. Everyone who loved and supported Ishi was there.

'Let Ishi compete,' Adya started chanting. 'Let Ishi compete!'

Ishi's mother joined in and so did Adya's mum. Soon the entire coachload of friends and family were chanting along too.

'Let Ishi compete! Let Ishi compete!'

The competitors noticed the commotion on the beach.

'What's going on?' they asked.

Adya's mum explained what had happened.

'That's not fair,' they said, joining in the chant.

'Let Ishi compete! Let Ishi compete!'

The judge made his way reluctantly up the beach to Ishi and her family.

'Let Ishi compete! Let Ishi compete!' the chants continued.

'Can you please leave?' the judge asked Ishi. 'We can't start the competition because the surfers are refusing to surf until we sort this out.'

'But I want a chance to prove what I can do,' Ishi said.

'It's the right thing to do,' one of the other surfers added.

'Fine,' the judge said, through gritted teeth.

The crowd cheered as Ishi ran to wthe water's edge with her board.

'I'm so proud of you,' her mother yelled as Ishi took to the water and paddled out.

Ishi lay on her board and shut her eyes. She felt the waves push her board up. She heard her aunty's voice in her head.

Breathe.

Ishi felt a warmth inside her chest as she spotted her friends on the beach. She rose up on the board, ready to surf her way to a win.